Sabbath Roots

VOLUME ONE

Sabbath Roots

SHELLY MILLER

PEREGRINATIO PRESS

ISBN 978-1-7334991-0-1

www.shellymillerwriter.com
Author is represented by Janet Grant,
Books and Such Literary Management.

Cover design by Harrison Miller.

Sabbath Society Circles logo, Copyright © Shelly Miller.
Created by Murielle Miller.

God insists over and over again that we move our eyes upward; from the small things that keep us stuck to the big, sweeping stories he is writing for us. As we rest, abide, listen, move out, and look up, we are surprised by the beauty that is cultivated, like stumbling onto a burning bush while wandering in the grocery store. Even in our disappointment we can still exclaim, "Glory!"

~Shelly Miller

CONTENTS

SABBATH SOCIETY CIRCLES

WHAT IS A SABBATH SOCIETY CIRCLE?

Sabbath Society Circles are designed to be autonomous, self-sustaining groups of people that meet routinely for storytelling, prayerful support, searching scripture, and sensing God's presence in the mundane of life. Circles are an outflow of the Sabbath Society online community, curated and led by Shelly Miller, author of Rhythms of Rest: Finding the Spirit of Sabbath in a Busy World.

WHY SABBATH SOCIETY CIRCLES?

While the world has advanced technologically and society is better connected, in fact most people feel more lonely, busy, and disconnected than ever before. Hustle and hurry are an attempt to fit into cultural norms for success while Sabbath is an invitation from God to pause, slow down, and remember this: you belong and are known by the Creator. While Sabbath-keeping is unique to each individual, weekly rest doesn't have to be a solitary endeavor. We cannot get to clarity on our own and Sabbath Society Circles provide an intimate, supportive, safe space for curating a rhythm of rest in the spirit of ease and togetherness. Empathy and compassion in the embrace of friendship does some deep soul work within us, providing spiritual growth and greater intimacy with Jesus.

WHAT A SABBATH SOCIETY CIRCLE IS:

A welcoming, supportive space for sharing openly in the spirit of love.

A compassionate and non-judgmental atmosphere for challenging the assumptions we tend to make about Sabbath.

A time set apart for exploring Sabbath as a rhythm of life.

A safe community of belonging and being known by God and others.

A place to share stories that inspire creativity in rest.

A time for listening to others and God before rushing to interject, problem solve, or create solutions.

An opportunity to cultivate deeper intimacy with Jesus and friendship with kindreds.

WHAT A SABBATH SOCIETY CIRCLE IS NOT:

A counseling or therapy session.

An opportunity for sharing your experiences as a method for fixing someone.

An academic exercise on the right or wrong theology of Sabbath-keeping.

About legalism—telling people what they should and should not do.

WHY SPIRITUAL DISCIPLINES?

"Superficiality is the curse of our age. The doctrine of instant satisfaction is a primary spiritual problem. The desperate need today is not for a greater number of intelligent people, or gifted people, but for deep people. The classical Disciplines of the spiritual life call us to move beyond surface living into the depths. They invite us to explore the inner caverns of the spiritual realm. They urge us to be the answer to a hollow world." ~Richard Foster, *Celebration of Disciplines*

OUR CORE VALUES

Friendship and Support: While serving as a Rest Mentor to a global community over the past six years, my experience reveals that most people struggle less with what Sabbath is and how to rest practically and more with achieving sovereign perspective--why God created Sabbath for us from the beginning. Until we discover rest as a core value of life, Sabbath remains elusive and impractical. And we cannot get to clarity alone. We need the perspective, support, and encouragement of others to persevere in finding rhythms of rest. In a chronically tired and lonely world, Sabbath Society Circles endeavor to fill that vacuum by creating safe, supportive communities.

Dispel Sabbath Myths: Many of us have been ill-informed or had negative experiences when it comes to Sabbath-keeping in the past. Sabbath Society Circles seek to stay away from legalistic mindsets and debating Sabbath theology. As we explore scripture together, learn from one another, the focus of the Circles will be based on the simplicity of the Gospel message--Christ crucified and resurrected, setting us free from Sabbath rules. Two predominant questions reign at the forefront of discussion: What has God done? And what is God doing now?

Deeper Intimacy with Jesus: Because most people struggle with achieving sovereign perspective versus situational clarity, practicing spiritual disciplines can lead to growth and vitality. Through Lectio Divina, worship, celebration, silence and listening prayer, Sabbath Society Circles create space to explore new practices in a loving and accepting environment. The primary requirement for achieving successful rest is a longing for more of God.

Creative Expression: Sabbath comes from the Hebrew word Shabbat which means to cease or stop; and to celebrate. The way we are created to rest is unique to each of us. What one person finds restful and rejuvenating, another person may find hard work and depleting. Each Sabbath Society Circle has a unique personality in the spirit of celebration. Circles can be gathered around a table with candles aflame or in a field after a morning walk; at a corporate conference table during lunch or on a blanket around a picnic lunch. Leaders will gather people in places and around activities that curate conversation, creativity, and inspire new ways to rest.

Now that you've read the visions and values for Sabbath Society Circles, gather your people, and let's begin a journey through the Old Testament passages where our Sabbath Roots began. May you discover God's heart in the creation of rest and find clarity in the throes of a supportive community.

INTRODUCTION

Congratulations! If you are holding this book in your hands it means you are serious about exploring how a rhythm of rest might look in your unique situation. Or at the very least, I assume you are curious to know more about Sabbath.

If you are a seasoned Sabbath-keeper but your practice has been solitary thus far, think of this book as a guide for cultivating a sense of belonging and being known by the people in your home, neighborhood, workplace, or village. With lots of intentional margin for taking notes, it is also a personal journal for capturing thoughts, questions, and ah-ha moments.

Sabbath Society Circles are curated around the world for the purpose of deepening intimacy with God and practicing rest within kindred community. Within the following pages, you will find answers to basic questions, capture the vision and core values for Sabbath Society Circles.

Each of the reflections are based on real letters written to an online global community called the Sabbath Society, founded in 2013. This first volume, based on Old Testament Sabbath passages, uses the historical spiritual practice of Lectio Divina as a place to begin your time together. The ancient practice is likened to "feasting on the Word"; taking small bites of scripture (lectio), chewing on it (meditatio), savoring the essence (oratio), and finally, digesting the Word until it becomes part of you (contemplatio). Over time, this form of meditative prayer has proven to increase a person's knowledge of Christ. While Lectio Divina is a deeply meaningful practice, it is not compulsory - each Sabbath Society Circle is autonomous and unique to the culture and personality of its members.

The questions can be used personally or as a group to stir deeper soul conversations about rest. The focus should not be completing all the questions but providing space for Circle members to make the most of each answer. Jesus used questions often throughout his life on earth as a way to achieve clarity among his followers. In the same way, the questions are here to help you think deeper, beyond the obvious, achieve new perspective, and transform tired thinking.

Because these topics have been explored among an existing online community in the past, there is an extravagance of riches in response from Sabbath Society members. As you read the anonymous quotes, use the viewpoints of others as a mirror to your own experience, a binocular view offering new perspective, or as jumping off point for exploring Sabbath more intimately.

Lastly, the closing prayers can be read aloud or quietly to yourself. The intent of the written prayers is to cultivate an atmosphere of listening prayer. In John 10:27, Jesus said, "My sheep listen to my voice; I know them, and they follow me." Listening prayer emphasizes listening over talking and hearing over formulating thought. Rather than thinking about God or talking to God, a listening posture allows a busy mind to settle and the heart to engage. Peace and clarity are often the result.

As you gather with your Circle in the spirit of ease and togetherness, I pray that your conversations will be rich, your perspective about rest will expand, intimacy with God will deepen, and new friendships will blossom. May you leave your Circle knowing you are deeply loved and fully known, returning more rested each time you meet again.

Resting with you,

Shelly

We were grounded so we could experience holy ground.

001: BEGIN AGAIN
{GENESIS 2:1-3}

The hope of starting over or beginning from a different place can carry us into new things with expectancy. But it's the inevitable disruptions that test our resolve. How we respond when life interrupts projected plans makes all the difference, especially when it comes to Sabbath-keeping. Those who persevere in times of uncertainty are certain to find rhythms of rest that last, even if it takes a while!

As the New Year began, we didn't envision being grounded – me sick in bed and my husband H in a tiny aisle seat on a plane. On Friday, as I pressed 'send' on my Sabbath Society weekly letter, I was experiencing a high fever, chills, and body aches; a full onslaught of influenza. While I was in bed shivering under a pile of blankets, H was packing his suitcase in preparation for an unexpected transatlantic flight back to the United States, after he received sad news that one of our spiritual fathers had passed. Staring at the ceiling, the words I had written in *Rhythms of Rest* came back to me.

"I'm dictating a forced rest. The unplanned vacant space seated in a doctor's reception area or during a train commute; while you are seated in an airport terminal or strapped in for a road trip; these are armchair altars for cultivating relationship with me. I'm creating windows of time for the overflow of your life to spill out and become a love offering. Trust me."[1]

We trusted God with the crappy timing of my getting sick. We trusted Him for finances we didn't have to pay for last minute plane tickets.

We trusted God to get H back to London in time for a meeting he had to lead fresh off the plane, jet lagged. We trusted Jesus to look after the health of our son and protect H's body from the stress of air travel. And all that trust led to this conclusion: We were grounded so we could experience holy ground.

As I kept the mattress on my side of the bed warm with worship and listening prayer, H crisscrossed the Atlantic and God spoke with us uniquely and intimately about similar things though physical distance separated us. Though a forced halt from routine wasn't what we would've chosen for ourselves, the unforeseen situation allowed for our faith to grow and discernment to deepen. The outcome of a stressful situation led to hearing God's small voice with clarity.

"We can interpret interruptions as roadblocks to peace or as moments for deepening relationship, trusting in the path God dictates." (Page 102)

How you respond is everything.

READ

Thus the heavens and the earth were finished, and all the host of them. And on the seventh day God finished his work that he had done, and he rested on the seventh day from all his work that he had done. So God blessed the seventh day and made it holy, because on it God rested from all his work that he had done in creation.
Genesis 2:1-3

MEDITATE

Take a few minutes to meditate on the words in the passage. Are there particular phrases or specific words standing out? Share what is being highlighted for you personally with your Circle. For further insight, ponder the questions and insert your perspective in the conversation.

How do you define holy?

The Hebrew word for holy is *qodesh* and means apartness, set-apartness, separateness, sacredness. In the New Testament, the word for holy is *hagios* and means set apart, reverent, sacred, and worthy of veneration. According to these definitions, what makes time holy for you?

How would it look for you to make time holy this week?

What keeps you from creating a rhythm of rest?

PRAY

Sit in silence for listening prayer. As you wait on God, allow what is on your mind to settle and what is hidden in the heart to surface.

CONTEMPLATE

Write down whatever comes to mind in the whitespace below. It can be a word, sentence, question, scripture verse, random thought, or image. Nothing is insignificant and everything is useful for capturing God's still small voice. When appropriate, share what comes from that time in your Circle. Perhaps what is discerned through listening prayer will be a gift for someone in the room.

Closing Prayer

Lord Jesus, may we all acquire discernment about interruptions -- less as disappointment and more as divinely placed. The armchair altars of mundane life can become holy ground we didn't expect. An opportunity to remember that "in Christ all the fullness of the Deity lives in bodily form, and in Christ you have been brought to fullness. He is the head over every power and authority." What more do we need? Thank you, Jesus for reminding us of your holiness and declaring time as holy and set apart. Amen!

RESPONSES FROM THE SABBATH SOCIETY

I don't think I know what Holy "is". However, I'm good at recognizing what it's "not". I'd like to switch my focus and look for the Holy in my life and offer it as a gift, rather than labeling all the ways I fall short.

What makes time Holy? My first sentence was: He makes time Holy. I am in awe how He is making every moment Holy - I should say how He is making me aware of His Holy! 'Tis so sweet to trust in Jesus, just to take Him at His Word.

At the end of your letter, you asked what holy means. When I looked it up, the phrase that lingered was "whole or intact". I suppose that helped me see our Sabbath keeping as a way of counteracting being divided. Our work week, the chaos of the world and our own striving can cut up our lives into slivers. The Sabbath pause/reset brings us back together, to our whole selves and to relying on God first and foremost. It's a reunion! – one you have taught me I can celebrate in tiny rhythms all week long.

I think of holy as set apart by God for his use and glory. So, making time holy in our home might look like activities that we wouldn't do on a typical day that are restful and worshipful (set apart).

*Sabbath is a clarifier
for who we are
and what we worship.*

002: CLARIFYING CONVICTIONS
{GENESIS 18: 1-8}

In London, our church provides four services on Sunday to meet the needs of our diverse, urban population: two in the morning and two in the evening. Sunday is a work day for my Vicar husband so generally, H is present at two of the four worship gatherings every week.

In the winter months, by 6:30pm, London is dark, cold, damp and quiet. While he's putting on his coat and scarf to brave the walk back to church, I'm tucked under blankets on the couch, holding a page turner and munching on freshly made popcorn (with lots of salt and a sprinkle of parmesan). It takes a great deal of conviction for me to leave the warm cocoon I've created to make the trek back to church a second time.

I haven't been in months which means I'm not very convicted. Or I'm in denial. But my lack of enthusiasm about going out in the cold isn't only about enjoying a cozy respite. For me, Sabbath ends when H walks out the door. Sunday night is also for catching up--washing dirty dishes, ironing shirts, responding to emails, and making an online grocery order. All that productivity would be lost to corporate worship, right?

Okay, wait a minute. I read the absurdity in that sentence. What could be more important than worship?

Well, maybe that's the point. If we were to say this sentence out loud:

_____ is more important than spending time with Jesus (folding laundry, tidying the house, clearing the inbox, watching Netflix) perhaps the absurdity of our busyness would become a revelation!

Last Sunday, conviction walked me back through the big blue doors of St. Barnabas Church because I'm desperate for more of God in my life. I decided all those chores could wait because worship in community and practicing the presence of God in a posture of listening is obviously a better use of my time. And you'll never guess what happened.

Someone who didn't know I was sitting in the crowd (because I'm usually not there on Sunday night!) shared about an epiphany she had after reading last week's Sabbath Society letter. God met her intimately through the words, bringing peace and comfort to a challenging season. She also declared to everyone listening, "Go buy *Rhythms of Rest* and sign up for the Sabbath Society letters!"

I was so flabbergasted by the unexpected testimony, the couple seated next to me jokingly asked if I had paid her to do it.

It wasn't that my ego was stroked in her declaration as much as it felt like a kiss on the cheek from God. The public affirmation felt like a personal acknowledgement from God for trusting Him with my time rather than trusting in myself to get things accomplished. Our little decisions have big consequences.

Sabbath is a clarifier for who we are and what we worship.

READ

And the Lord appeared to him (Abraham) by the oaks of Mamre, as he sat at the door of his tent in the heat of the day. He lifted up his eyes and looked, and behold, three men were standing in front of him. When he saw them, he ran from the tent door to meet them and bowed himself to the earth and said, "O Lord, if I have found favor in your sight, do not pass by your servant. Let a little water be brought, and wash your feet, and rest yourselves under the tree, while I bring a morsel of bread, that you may refresh yourselves, and after that you may pass on—since you have come to your servant." So they said, "Do as you have said." And Abraham went quickly into the tent to Sarah and said, "Quick! Three seahs of fine flour! Knead it, and make cakes." And Abraham ran to the herd and took a calf, tender and good, and gave it to a young man, who prepared it quickly. Then he took curds and milk and the calf that he had prepared, and set it before them. And he stood by them under the tree while they ate.
Genesis 18:1-8

MEDITATE

Take a few minutes to meditate on the words in the passage. Are there particular phrases or specific words standing out? Share what is being highlighted for you personally with your Circle. For further insight, ponder the questions and insert your perspective in the conversation.

This Sabbath passage echoes the grounding due to interruption that we talked about in the last reflection. How does this passage translate for you?

What does Abraham's response to interruption teach us about hospitality in rest? What does it reveal about relationships, trust, character and humility?

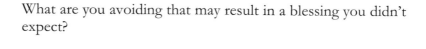

What are you avoiding that may result in a blessing you didn't expect?

It is said that how you spend your minutes is how you live your life. Make a list of how you spent your time today. Summarize in a headline what your life is saying to you.

PRAY

Spend a few minutes in silence and wait on the Lord.

CONTEMPLATE

Write down whatever comes to mind in the whitespace below. It can be a word, sentence, question, scripture verse, random thought, or image. Nothing is insignificant and everything is useful for capturing God's still small voice. When appropriate, share what comes from that time in your Circle. Perhaps what is discerned through listening prayer will be a gift for someone in the room.

CLOSING PRAYER

Lord, when I am prone to choose comfort in the familiar and fear scarcity over trust, sober me with your perspective. Take me back to all the times when you have showed up in the past and provided what I needed in the grace of your perfect timing. Push me past self-reliance into a reliance on you; God-reliant rather than a reliance on what I produce as a measurement of my worth. Amen!

RESPONSES FROM THE SABBATH SOCIETY

Abraham's hospitality showed his devotion to the service of God, who came to him through the three visitors. One definition I found for holy was "devoted to the service of God." I also thought about Isaiah 58:13-14 and how Sabbath invites us to honor God in the time He gives us, to orient and organize our schedules out of devotion to Him, seeking first to honor Him and finding our delight in Him as a result.

I see abundance in that passage—that when God grounds us, He supplies what we need for the duration of time we are resting (or removed from activity). That passage speaks of "enough"—no scarcity at all, but enough to meet our every need, whether it's a two-day, two-week, or two-year supply. Whatever our need, with God, there is always enough . . . in fact, so much, that we don't need to go out and scrounge around, looking to our own meager resources to find satisfaction. We can stay put and stay grounded just where He has placed us, because in the end, He is always enough!

This passage says Abraham was outside the tent during the hottest part of the day. I imagine him choosing to step outside, step away from the heat inside and sit for a moment to rest in the shade. From a place of rest in verse 2 it says, "He looked up and noticed..." This is what rest does for us! I pray that I can continue to choose rest and rhythm this year. Seeking this God-given balance so my perspective changes and my eyes may continually be lifted off myself and able to see others and the "interruptions" around me.

Sabbath is a weekly reminder that we are not invincible, and Jesus is our conqueror. We overcome through the blood of the Lamb, not the blood, sweat, and tears of our hard work.

003: REFUSAL AS SELF-HARM
{EXODUS 16: 28-29}

Last night, I hobbled down thirty-two winding steps to the ground floor and joined my family for a meal at the dining room table rather than eating alone from the tray table propped over my lap in bed. A women's small group from church hosted a generous collection and delivered five pre-made meals as I convalesce from the flu. I can still taste the sweet sticky icing swiped from the top of a piece of gourmet carrot cake. Just what the doctor ordered to bring health and vigor back into my lackluster week.

Across the hall from my office turned recovery room, my son has been lying in bed too, recovering from the flu. Passing time on electronic devices in between naps, we commiserated with moans, greetings, and goodnight sayings through cracks in doors kept slightly ajar. Today was his first day back to school after missing a full week of progress and the first time we've gathered at the dinner table together since being sick.

"I think people here must treat the flu differently than we're used to," Harrison observed as an expat.

He went on to tell us how kids were coming to school in droves with body aches, chills, and fever. Sitting in classrooms when they should be in bed, playing sports in the cold while aching from head to toe, as if denial will somehow will the body back to health. Not only are the kids compromising their own bodies but the health of their classmates. His account has haunted me ever since.

To treat in a harmful, injurious, or offensive way is the definition for abuse. We don't think of refusing to rest as a kind of abuse we inflict upon ourselves, but it is. Before I cast the first stone though, I should take personal inventory.

How many times have I rushed the healing process of a virus in the past, only to have a setback?

How many times have I passed over Sabbath, to do instead of simply be, and compromised the health of my soul?

How many times have I rushed to produce from fear and denied His still small voice?

How many times have I abused the time God gives by thinking it was mine to do with as I wish?

Sabbath is a weekly reminder that we are not invincible, and Jesus is our conqueror. We overcome through the blood of the Lamb, not the blood, sweat, and tears of our hard work.

READ

"The Lord asked Moses, 'How long will these people refuse to obey my commands and instructions? They must realize that the Sabbath is the Lord's gift to you. That is why he gives you a two-day supply [of manna] on the sixth day, so there will be enough for two days. On the Sabbath day you must each stay in your place. Do not go out to pick up food on the seventh day.'"
Exodus 16:28-29

MEDITATE

Take a few minutes to meditate on the words in the passage. Are there particular phrases or specific words standing out? Share what is being highlighted for you personally with your Circle. For further insight, ponder the questions and insert your perspective in the conversation.

What do these verses tell you about God's intention for the Sabbath?

Think of a time when the fear of scarcity overwhelmed your plans to rest. What was the result?

What is it that you feel you don't have enough of right now?

How might God be challenging you to trust him with uncertainty?

Ask God to give you faith for manna in an area of life that feels especially vulnerable.

PRAY

Spend a few minutes in silence and wait on the Lord.

CONTEMPLATE

Write down whatever comes to mind in the whitespace below. It can be a word, sentence, question, scripture verse, random thought, or image. Nothing is insignificant and everything is useful for capturing God's still small voice. When appropriate, share what comes from that time in your Circle. Perhaps what is discerned through listening prayer will be a gift for someone in the room.

CLOSING PRAYER

Lord, forgive me for the times when I have taken the details of life into my own hands and pushed you aside. I need you more than I need self-sufficiency. Help me to see that not choosing the gift of Sabbath is a kind of abuse I'm unintentionally inflicting upon myself. May I see the choice of Sabbath as a healing kindness I extend to myself. Whatever it is that I think I have to accomplish outside of your grace is an idol replacing your presence. And I don't want that. I want more of you. May our rest this week reflect worship and adoration, the kindness of glorifying God with praise and thankfulness for the great abundance He provides. Amen.

RESPONSES FROM THE SABBATH SOCIETY

God's message to Moses reminded me of what I am learning about trusting Him to rest. I am busy building up a small business and I have had that feeling that I must check every email immediately, meet every deadline and put all my energies into working as much as possible to get a good reputation with my clients. However, I recently realized God was challenging me to trust Him to take time off too. I made a decision not to do any paid work on a Sunday, trusting Him to help me fit what I had to do in the other 6 days. I then took the (for me very brave) step further and decided to not even check my business email account on a Sunday. I put a footnote on my automatic signature to that effect and I am slowly beginning to enjoy the feeling of freedom it brings. Small steps, but He does, indeed, know what's best for us. Hallelujah.

"They must realize that the Sabbath is the Lord's gift to you. That is why he gives you a two-day supply [of manna] on the sixth day, so there will be enough for two days." He supplies, yet how often I operate based on that principle of scarcity, especially when it comes to time. He gives with intention, providing what we need—what I need. I know this, but still find myself in the trap of believing I need to provide it for myself. I don't. God says so.

Sabbath is a gift. It is a reminder not only to see His abundance, but to rest in it & enjoy His abundance.

We cannot extend grace to others if we are not willing to give grace to ourselves first.

004: THE KINDNESS OF REST
{EXODUS 20: 8-11}

The last time we met, we processed how a lack of rest can be a kind of abuse we inflict upon ourselves without intent. This time, let's explore kindness from God's perspective. How does being kind to yourself look when time is limited for rest?

In *Sacred Rhythms*, Ruth Haley Barton writes, "Something about being gracious and accepting and gentle with ourselves at least once a week enables us to be more gracious and accepting and gentle with others. There is a freedom that comes from being who we are in God and resting in God that eventually enables us to bring something truer to the world than all of our doing. Sabbath-keeping helps us to live within our limits, because on the Sabbath, in many different ways, we allow ourselves to be the creature in the presence of our Creator. We touch something more real in ourselves and others than what any of us is able to produce. We touch our very being in God."[2]

How does this quote resonate with you?

For me, being patient, tender and gentle with myself looks like walking past piles of tissues and dirty socks lying on the floor, reaching for my Bible, and meditating on scripture, fully attentive for more than a few minutes. Extending grace to myself looks like an uncharacteristic mid-day nap rather than getting dressed and running errands. As I continue to gain strength and recover from illness, I am tempted to push myself back into productivity as a prescription for feeling better about myself.

When I let go of lofty standards and accept current limitations, I discover that what Haley Barton writes about is true! When I extend grace to myself through the kind choice of rest, compassion wells up within me for those who are chronically ill, bed-ridden, or just stopped from living life as usual. I begin to see the world with Gods eyes, translate life through a Sabbath heart, and kindness becomes a work of art.

We cannot extend grace to others if we are not willing to give grace to ourselves first.

Surprisingly, an enforced Sabbath through an unforeseen illness mutated into a beautiful opportunity to fall in love with Jesus again. Because the more I spend time quietly with God, the more my heart yearns to be with him. The more I seek him through prayer, everything I assumed as important becomes impertinent. The more I discern his presence and purpose, the more I want his will and nothing else. You?

READ

Remember the Sabbath day, to keep it holy. Six days you shall labor, and do all your work, but the seventh day is a Sabbath to the Lord your God. On it you shall not do any work, you, or your son, or your daughter, your male servant, or your female servant, or your livestock, or the sojourner who is within your gates. For in six days the Lord made heaven and earth, the sea, and all that is in them, and rested on the seventh day. Therefore the Lord blessed the Sabbath day and made it holy.
Exodus 20:8-11

"Tell the people of Israel: 'Be careful to keep my Sabbath day, for the Sabbath is a sign of the covenant between me and you from generation to generation. It is given so you may know that I am the Lord, who makes you holy. You must keep the Sabbath day, for it is a holy day for you. . . The people of Israel must keep the Sabbath day by observing it from generation to generation. This is a covenant obligation for all time".
Exodus 31:13-14, 16

MEDITATE

Take a few minutes to meditate on the words in the passage. Are there particular phrases or specific words standing out? Share what is being highlighted for you personally with your Circle. For further insight, ponder the questions and insert your perspective in the conversation.

How is Sabbath a choice of kindness to yourself? And kindness extended to others?

What was God communicating through a choice of rest on the seventh day when He didn't need rest to function?

The opposite of abuse is kindness. Create a list of synonyms for kindness and identify words that people would use to describe you. Or take turns proclaiming words of kindness over the members in your Circle.

Identify a time when you were patient, tender, and gentle with yourself in the past week. When did you extend grace over judgment? When were you charitable with yourself at a time when you would normally be prone to condemnation?

PRAY

Spend a few minutes in silence and wait on the Lord.

CONTEMPLATE

Write down whatever comes to mind in the whitespace below. It can be a word, sentence, question, scripture verse, random thought, or image. Nothing is insignificant and everything is useful for capturing God's still small voice. When appropriate, share what comes from that time in your Circle. Perhaps what is discerned through listening prayer will be a gift for someone in the room.

CLOSING PRAYER

Jesus, may I extend permission for rest to myself in the same way I encourage the people I love to rest. Help me to see what self-kindness looks like. Show me the difference between kindness and selfishness. Teach me how to be a caretaker of my mind, body, soul, and spirit. God, may I glorify you in the way I choose to Sabbath. Amen!

RESPONSES FROM THE SABBATH SOCIETY

This is so true. I find that on the Sabbath I am much more gentle with myself and in turn I feel like it's the best day of the week with my kids. Their attitudes are calmer and we seem to all flow a bit easier. Of course, that's not always the case because they are 4 and 2, but I do see the connection. Being kind to myself today by laying in bed and watching the IF Gathering stream. No dishes. No laundry folding. No picking up after the kids. Resting now will help me to love on others at our small group in a few hours as well.

Recently I have developed vertigo and a condition in my dominant arm which requires me to wear a long arm brace. I am mostly unable to use that hand. Normally I would fret over things I can't do or have left unfinished. Instead I have given myself permission to live within these limitations. I am being gentle and kind to myself, resting in the faithfulness of Jesus knowing He is gently caring for me. I have been able to ask for help which has never been easy. It feels good to care for myself and trust that Jesus knows.

As someone who suffered abuse it is hard to care for myself in a way where I am kind, gentle, loving, easy-going (and any other synonym) on myself. Why should I? Something that has been instilled into me as I was growing up was that I never reached the mark, I was always second best, I deserved the abuse I got and that it was normal, so I guess in the back of my mind I'm unintentionally still doing this through not focusing on myself, hence the reason why I am always unwell. I have this feeling that if I let my guard down, or if I just "let go" I have failed.

A covenant, to me, sounds quite harsh and something that is really formal. I think I prefer to see it as a bond or a promise which sounds gentler, and after all this is what I need to be... gentle on myself. As for loving and belonging... these are so connected with each other. Once we start to acknowledge who we are in Christ and love ourselves we will then start to feel accepted and belong.

Sabbath brings desire to the surface, shedding the false self to expose what is truest about you.

005: DESIRING GOD
{LEVITICUS 23:3}

In a lavish turn of fortune and the invitation of friends, my family experienced the perfect Sabbath repose at a charming old world estate in Scotland. Though the weather was frightfully cold, afternoon walks in wellies in the woods meant a deserved opportunity afterward to cozy up in front of a blazing fireplace with a warm cuppa in hand. And of course, what would afternoon tea be without a slice of cake? Lounging for long periods, cat naps at intervals, lingering in conversation surrounded by candlelight and crystal at dinner—this atmosphere pervaded our decadent getaway.

As you can probably imagine, there was a lot of sighing and slumping of shoulders going on as we packed up to leave and drive back. Back to preparing grocery lists, culling a full inbox, and taking care of household responsibilities. Quietness enveloped the car as we drove down narrow country lanes cutting through rolling hills dotted with grazing sheep. When we arrived back to our London terrace house, H finally came down with the flu just as Harrison and I had recovered.

Truthfully, the sadness we experienced as we left Scotland has become my mood every week once the sun sets on a 24-hour rest period. I long for that kind of Sabbath intimacy to continue. I'm often expectant because God's presence seems different, multiplied in closeness somehow, much like what the Jews refer to as a second soul that comes for a special visit on Sabbath.

Sabbath brings desire to the surface, shedding the false self to expose what is truest about you.

Being present to centuries of family history in the place where we visited was inspiring and rooted something magically meaningful within all of us. But it is easy to assume our identity stems from ancestral history, titles, failures, missteps, personality type, and vocation. In rest, we discover that the truest thing about us is our longing for God. As we stop and listen for His still small voice, desire floats quietly through the noise in our head, and peace comes like a soft gentle breeze, unobtrusive and refreshing.

What do you desire from God right now?

We love because he first loved us (I John 4:19) but sometimes I admit I walk around thinking that if I love God first, then he will reciprocate.

But God longs for us first.

He initiates relationship with you.

Everything originates with a Person; not your plans, processes and productivity.

Isn't that a relief?

If spiritual desire is stirring within you, then God is at work wooing you; reminding you of who you are when you've tricked yourself into thinking who you are is what you do.

READ

You have six days each week for your ordinary work, but the seventh day is a Sabbath day of complete rest, an official day for holy assembly. It is the Lord's Sabbath day, and it must be observed wherever you live.
Leviticus 23:3

MEDITATE

Take a few minutes to meditate on the words in the passage. Are there particular phrases or specific words standing out? Share what is being highlighted for you personally with your Circle. For further insight, ponder the questions and insert your perspective in the conversation.

What does the phrase in this passage "complete rest" mean for you?

What is the difference between complete and perfect?

Perhaps complete is a good marker to use when we determine time set apart for rest, keeping the temptation to produce at bay. What does giving your complete attention to God in Sabbath look like for you this week?

How might you be complicating rest with rigid rules?

How would you describe Sabbath-keeping last week? Complete? Or half-hearted?

What could you do differently this week to make complete rest possible?

PRAY

Spend a few minutes in silence and wait on the Lord.

CONTEMPLATE

Write down whatever comes to mind in the whitespace below. It can be a word, sentence, question, scripture verse, random thought, or image. Nothing is insignificant and everything is useful for capturing God's still small voice. When appropriate, share what comes from that time in your Circle. Perhaps what is discerned through listening prayer will be a gift for someone in the room.

CLOSING PRAYER

Lord, you know I don't have the luxury of getting away to a nice peaceful repose regularly. But I want to experience that regular feeling of inner rest in my unique context. Come Lord Jesus, into my every day walking around life. Reveal your presence to me. Give me the grace to linger long in conversation with you. Show me how to make time celebratory with what I already have right in front of me. Thank you that complete rest isn't about trying harder but hardly trying to produce. Amen!

RESPONSES FROM THE SABBATH SOCIETY

These words right here: "If spiritual desire is stirring within you, then God is at work wooing you; reminding you of who you are when you've tricked yourself into thinking who you are is what you do", were a friendly breeze across my brow. I'm not certain exactly how this applies to my general sense of heart and soul-unease, but I know it does. There's a stirring there, a spiritual one. There's a lack of certainty over just what will happen next. There's a knowing that I'm waiting for something, but I don't know exactly what. I suppose your words ring with the whisper that it will be okay, that it already is okay, and that I'm not alone.

I never thought I could have peace at the end of longing until I sat still with Peace himself. 'Be still and know' isn't just a great meme, it is the way to becoming our truest selves in the presence of God.

I went to sleep spent, frustrated that after four days of working in my home, I seem no closer to order than I was on Monday morning. The chaos is no more than usual, the fruit of a family living full lives in a space that is their home. It just feels daily so unproductive and unimportant. My head knows this is not so, but my heart can't quite agree. So today, I'm setting aside the tasks to focus on Jesus and my heart. Maybe not all day, maybe just an hour or two. Your words give me hope that in turning my eyes on Jesus, the soul gets what it needs, and the body is able to again work with purpose and cheerful intention.

I'm about to spend my Sabbath in a 5-star hotel at rock bottom price! I'm slowly learning how to look after myself and enjoy the weekend rather than use it for recovery only (how sad is that!).

Sometimes I guess, we don't realize how deeply wounded we are in certain ways: because we are strong warriors we can soldier on, but God is so loving, wanting us to be so deeply restored and complete in Him, that He draws us into a season of Sabbath solitude in which to heal. I can't explain all the things He is doing because it is good and hard, but Sabbath has truly become about healing for me.

Think of Sabbath as rescue from the false self you have believed is the true you.

006: IT'S YOUR JUBILEE!
{LEVITICUS 25:1-16 AND LEVITICUS 27:24}

As Christians we learn to say that our identity is in Christ and not what we do; it rolls off the tongue like responding, "fine" when someone asks, "How are you?" But when identity flows from what you do and what you do every day is removed, the sum of what you get is yourself without what you produce. No titles, influence, or tangible evidence of your place in the world. And that can be scary for a whole lot of us. Walk into a room of strangers and the first question to break awkwardness is, "What do you do?" How do you answer during uncertain seasons?

Think of Sabbath as rescue from the false self you have believed is the true you. Sabbath is the sure axis making the turning wheels of your life balanced and sturdy for what lies ahead. Sometimes a lengthy sabbatical can be a form of detox from the mindsets and routines that have kept your heart on auto-pilot.

Living as an expat in London is a dream come true but realizing that dream was preceded by a painful, fallow season. At times, I translated the uncertainty of a forced sabbatical while we waited for visas as God's method for my great undoing. But Sabbath provided rescue.

What began as a jubilant leap of faith in leaving a job, paycheck, influence, and work we loved for a ministry call to London, mutated into bureaucracy, delays in selling a house, and our bank account dwindling; of stagnating rather than blowing a trumpet in celebration.

I was a modern-day echo of the Israelites moaning to Moses, "Surely you didn't call us to London only to leave us bereft and poverty-stricken."

And then one day in August, during my birthday week, I was standing in front of the bathroom mirror when my H said something memorable. "This is your year of jubilee! You should see this time of waiting as a gift to celebrate." As is often the case, his words brought the clarity I desperately needed that day.

As I ponder our Sabbath scriptures from Leviticus, this is my great theological conclusion. The year of jubilee is basically a do-over; a year of God declaring, "Stop what you're doing. Take a load off! It is time for you to remember some important truths that have been lost in the detritus of your busyness." Of course, the year of jubilee is so much deeper than this elementary explanation.

Back in the day, when Moses was leading the Israelites into the Promised Land, God issued some stipulations. While the Israelites were to observe Sabbath every seventh day, the land itself would observe Sabbath every seven years. When the rhythm of seven years accrued seven times, the land and the people would rest together.

Most of us only allot a few weeks on the calendar for time off from work, but God was giving them one entire year off with added benefits! Land used as collateral for unpaid debt was returned to the original owner. All the back-breaking, finger-splitting work of sowing, reaping, and gathering was put on hiatus. Slaves and prisoners were set free to return to their families. Can you imagine the celebration and all that trumpet blowing?

What if your boss walked into your cubicle and said, "I'm paying off your debts, take the year off and enjoy. Live off your savings and we'll see you in twelve months." How would you respond? Would you go out and celebrate? Or be tempted to fill that whitespace up with more doing?

Initially, that kind of margin sounds like a dream come true. But, as I learned a few years ago, once the newness of having an extravagance of whitespace wears off, waking up without a purpose can challenge our identity.

You may ask, "What shall we eat in the seventh year if we do not plant or harvest our crops?" And God will respond, "I will send you such a blessing in the sixth year that the land will yield enough for three years. While you plant during the eighth year, you will eat from the old crop and will continue to eat from it until the harvest of the ninth year comes in." (Leviticus 25: 20-22, NIV)

Sabbath reminds us that when we take our hands off of creation, we become fertile soul for Christ to cultivate a life that is ultimately fruitful and fulfilling. Will you trust me to provide for you? is the clarion call of God to us when he created the Sabbath.

My year of jubilee wasn't without wrestling. I wondered daily how we would eat and stay current on bills; how we would explain to our children that our decision wasn't careless. I vacillated between hope and despair. Despair when my mind began focusing on circumstances and hope when I remembered how God has been faithful in the past.

READ

The Lord spoke to Moses on Mount Sinai, saying, "Speak to the people of Israel and say to them, When you come into the land that I give you, the land shall keep a Sabbath to the Lord. For six years you shall sow your field, and for six years you shall prune your vineyard and gather in its fruits, but in the seventh year there shall be a Sabbath of solemn rest for the land, a Sabbath to the Lord. You shall not sow your field or prune your vineyard. You shall not reap what grows of itself in your harvest, or gather the grapes of your undressed vine. It shall be a year of solemn rest for the land. The Sabbath of the land shall provide food for you, for yourself and for your male and female slaves and for your hired worker and the sojourner who lives with you, and for your cattle and for the wild animals that are in your land: all its yield shall be for food.

"You shall count seven weeks of years, seven times seven years, so that the time of the seven weeks of years shall give you forty-nine years. Then you shall sound the loud trumpet on the tenth day of the seventh month. On the Day of Atonement you shall sound the trumpet throughout all your land. And you shall consecrate the fiftieth year, and proclaim liberty throughout the land to all its inhabitants. It shall be a jubilee for you, when each of you shall return to his property and each of you shall return to his clan. That fiftieth year shall be a jubilee for you; in it you shall neither sow nor reap what grows of itself nor gather the grapes from the undressed vines. For it is a jubilee. It shall be holy to you. You may eat the produce of the field.

"In this year of jubilee each of you shall return to his property. And if you make a sale to your neighbor or buy from your neighbor, you shall not wrong one another. You shall pay your neighbor according to the number of years after the jubilee, and he shall sell to you according to the number of years for crops. If the years are many, you shall increase the price, and if the years are few, you shall reduce the price, for it is the number of the crops that he is selling to you.
Leviticus 25: 1-16

In the year of jubilee the field shall return to him from whom it was bought, to whom the land belongs as a possession.
Leviticus 27:24

54

MEDITATE

Take a few minutes to meditate on the words in the following passage. Are there particular phrases or specific words standing out? Share what is being highlighted for you personally with your Circle. For further insight, ponder the questions and insert your perspective in the conversation.

> What if the barren seasons of our lives are a kind of permission from being driven by externals to being led internally by the love and kindness of Jesus?

> What if the fallowness we experience in the fields of our work and relationships are a clarion call declaring, "It's your time to cultivate a healthy soul, to remember that my love is enough for you."

> What are you doing now that will sustain seasons of fallowness?

> How might deposits of rest now provide a harvest in the future?

How does time off without plans or projected purpose translate for you?

What is hemming you in right now?

What are you waiting to be free from so you can finally live fully?

What if you were to set free your idealized version of rest? How might that freedom lead you to live the life God has for you right now?

PRAY

Spend a few minutes in silence and wait on the Lord.

CONTEMPLATE

Write down whatever comes to mind in the whitespace below. It can be a word, sentence, question, scripture verse, random thought, or image. Nothing is insignificant and everything is useful for capturing God's still small voice. When appropriate, share what comes from that time in your Circle. Perhaps what is discerned through listening prayer will be a gift for someone in the room.

CLOSING PRAYER

Lord, forgive me for translating the gift of rest as a dreaded time period creating anxiety rather than a celebration of your faithfulness. Help me to see rest the way you created it—for my good and the good of your creation. When I am prone to produce as a measurement of my worth and value, build within me a reservoir of trust as I Sabbath. Give me eyes to translate fallowness in my life as timely rescue from self-reliance. May the time I set aside as holy rest be a rightful and just restoring of what busyness has taken from me. Amen!

Responses from the Sabbath Society

"What if you were to set free your idealized version of rest so you can realize the life God has for you right now?' The thought came to me this past week as I have battled the flu - I don't think I really know HOW to rest. I'm praying that the Lord will show me how to rest my body and my soul. It's His gift to us.

Jubilee struck a chord with me. I am celebrating (and/or enduring) a jubilee year. As I approached my 50th birthday, I felt the Spirit pressing the idea of marking off space for a fallow time. My life is in transition in a myriad of ways and the thought seemed crazy this time last year. It has been like moving from the hustle and bustle of city life to the wide-open spaces of the countryside. The truth is, I haven't handled it all that well. I've chafed against the emptiness, I've fallen into fear and frustration, and spent quite a bit of time whining to God that I will never be useful again. But I needed this time to just be with my Father; time to recognize the places where my roles and responsibilities have overshadowed my sense of well-being in relationship with the One who holds my life.

I have resigned from my job to take a break and regain my health. I've never been blessed with a strong constitution, and shingles at Christmas knocked me for six. I'm going to take a year out to rest, see my family, travel, and do some voluntary work. I was fine with it until this morning, and then the doubts started whispering. Well, your message reminds me of what I learned when I was ill with a fever last week. As I woke up from a sweaty afternoon sleep, I saw - in a split second - this phase of my life between two places. God showed me that time is a different dimension for Him. We see it like 24 hours a day, but He sees eternity. His perception of time is completely different. He's in charge of all the details, even this sickness. The only thing He's not in charge of is my choice to love or be selfish.

The space between
where we have come and
where we are going is
God's rest.

007: FREE FROM NOSTALGIA
{DEUTERONOMY 5:15}

Lying alone on a lounge chair beside the pool, tears slide down my cheeks from underneath sunglasses. In less than 24 hours I'll be boarding a plane in Phoenix, headed to Ohio for a writing retreat before flying home. I've had two weeks of bliss, enjoying presence with family and predictable sunshine while the forecast is for snow in London. I'm sad about leaving brilliant blue skies and sun-kissed skin, but mostly, I'm grieving the imminent separation from my first born. I never know when our paths will intersect the next time. It could be months or even a year.

She is repeating my history. Driving from North Carolina to Phoenix on her own, Murielle relocated to her birthplace among family members, testing the waters of opportunity after a string of dead ends. Finding a job, peer community, and church, she is thriving in a new place.

Nearly three decades ago, in faith, I left home in Oklahoma to pursue a life in Phoenix, sight unseen, testing the waters of opportunity after a string of dead ends. Driving cross country alone, I arrived in Phoenix with hopeful aspirations and found a job, community, church, and eventually, a husband. But before marrying H, I lay face down on a lounge chair at the apartment pool with tears dripping onto the deck from underneath sunglasses. As I turned the pages of *Co-dependent No More*, I found emotional and spiritual health in the desert after surviving an insecure childhood.

Pilgrimage begins in the desert. We are enslaved to something, waiting to be set free, and walking toward the fulfillment of God's promises.

Life is a continual paradox of joy and suffering, lack and abundance, uncertain circumstances and the certainty of God's love. We tend to avoid suffering at all costs, but the wilderness is our Harvard and Yale in the discovery of true meaning and purpose in life. Without seasons of wandering in the desert, the promises of God can translate as impersonal idealism.

My tears flow from the grip of nostalgia that longs to hold on to a remnant of relationship with my daughter. But nostalgia keeps me stuck and living in the past, rather than letting go and moving forward in trust. My daughter's home is the same desert that shaped me into the mother I am to her today. And my home now is in London where God is doing a new work, shaping me into His likeness and preparing me for the unknowns that lie ahead.

The space between where we have come and where we are going is God's rest.

Sabbath came in the form of the ten commandments while the Israelites were wandering in the desert. And when life became uncertain, the Israelites were prone toward nostalgia, wishing for the certainty of the past even when the past wasn't God's best for them. Rest became a form of rescue—being rescued from yourself to be released into God's providence. Sabbath provided rescue from wishful thinking and perspective toward God's faithful provision.

READ

You shall remember that you were a slave in the land of Egypt, and the Lord your God brought you out from there with a mighty hand and an outstretched arm. Therefore the Lord your God commanded you to keep the Sabbath day.
Deuteronomy 5:15

MEDITATE

Take a few minutes to meditate on the words in the following passage. Are there particular phrases or specific words standing out? Share what is being highlighted for you personally with your Circle. For further insight, ponder the questions and insert your perspective in the conversation.

What mindset about rest from the past is keeping you stuck from moving into weekly Sabbath?

How is nostalgia keeping you from thriving today?

What situation do you need to release into God's trust in order to live free from inner unrest?

What new thing is God asking of you? Is there anything causing you to doubt his faithfulness?

What are the false narratives you are telling yourself that keep you from rest?

PRAY

Spend a few minutes in silence and wait on the Lord. Write down whatever comes to mind in the whitespace below. It can be a word, sentence, question, scripture verse, random thought, or image. Nothing is insignificant and everything is useful for capturing God's still small voice. When appropriate, share what comes from that time in your Circle. Perhaps what is discerned through listening prayer will be a gift for someone in the room.

Closing Prayer

Lord, forgive me when I retreat into the past as comfort for the fear of uncertainty. You are my only certainty. Thank you for being faithful when I am faithless. Show me when I am allowing nostalgia to become a stronghold—making decisions about life based on past experience, instead of allowing space for faith to grow. Reveal your presence amidst the unknowns. Cultivate within me a hope that is built on trust rather than self-reliance. I long to be led by your love rather than the love of my preferred outcomes. May I be wholly dependent upon you in all areas of life. Amen!

RESPONSES FROM THE SABBATH SOCIETY

I grew up in such a heavy works-based religion; I have been finding myself lately falling back into the mindset I grew up with. Wondering if I am doing this Jesus life the right way, if I am spending my time correctly and obediently, if I am allowed not to do something that I find completely depleting, and the thoughts are too much at times and don't stop coming. This week I was reminded of this verse, Deut. 5:15 to "remember" what God has already done for me. I cannot do anything on top of that and sometimes, most of the time, I need to give myself grace. I am called to a playful rest!

Thank you! I woke today in a bit of turmoil, wondering about future things and 'what if's', but in my quiet time I was reminded of the faithfulness of the Lord and the Hope that only HE can bring. To read your words are just another reminder of his constant presence and provision.

This is the first week of what I've coined my "healing sabbatical"; a minimum of 6 months rest and play - my husband's stipulations. Last fall, I received a difficult health diagnosis, which demanded that I make rest my first priority in order to heal and get better. Thirty years of trauma, stress and over working can really do a number on one's body. I'm learning this first hand. I'm so grateful for Rhythms of Rest and the Sabbath community, which helped lay foundations for all that this reality is requiring of me.

The truth will set you free from the myths believed about Sabbath.

008: THE GRITTY TRUTH
{2 CHRONICLES 36:21}

As an author, I can tell you that the writing life can be an isolating vocation. Most creatives wrestle alone with disappointments, and the assumption that we are the only one – the only one struggling with self-doubt, the only one unable to grow a platform, the only one suffering with rejection.

But as I listen to colleagues in various stages and ages of life, their stories become a revelation and comfort. Empathy does some good work within us to reveal the truth among the lies we tell ourselves. And sometimes hearing the truth from an outside voice is needed to move forward. The truth will set you free from the myths believed about Sabbath.

Endeavors toward Sabbath-keeping are often solitary. What we envision as hopeful transformation through rest can sometimes vanish under the actual work of preparing for rest. Because interruptions happen and they threaten to derail us from a Sabbath focus.

You might assume you are the only one who can't seem to make Sabbath work-- the only one who fails to prepare properly, the only one who struggles with focus, the only one unable to overcome interruptions. And as a kindred Sabbath-keeper, I'm offering you my shoulder because I want to dispel that untruth.

No one is immune from struggles with self-doubt, questioning purpose, and finding fulfillment in life. And no matter what age or stage of life, we all struggle with finding a rhythm of rest too. In Christ, Sabbath is possible for everyone, not because circumstances fall magically into place, but because we were created with a healthy dose of grit.

Grit means courage and resolve; strength of character. It is possible to summon courage and resolve to keep the faith despite life's disappointments. As gritty people, we can and will experience the riches of Sabbath.

Psychologist Angela Duckworth defines grit as "the ability to persevere in pursuing a future goal over a long period of time and not giving up… It is having stamina. It's sticking with your future, day-in, day-out, not just for the week, not just for the month, but for years and working really hard to make that future a reality. Grit is living life like it's a marathon, not a sprint."[3]

Think of Esther risking it all to save her people, Moses sacrificing quiet comfort to lead whining Israelites through the desert, Noah building an ark for decades before the rain fell, Daniel refusing to bow to idols, Mary giving birth to the Savior as a virgin. These people displayed grit when it wasn't popular to do so.

I want to be a person characterized by grit, not as someone who easily gives up, don't you?

Sabbath isn't a popular choice in today's busy climate of hurry, hustle and get those lists checked off quickly. Rest can seem more like a novelty than a gift from God's generous heart. If you feel that way, I want you to know that you are not alone. Keep going! Keep taking baby steps toward realizing your own unique rhythms of rest and one day, you'll find your stride; a gait that is unique to how God created you to amble, linger, and savor Sabbath.

Like those gritty heroes of the faith who paved the way for us, let's be people who overcome obstacles common to us and inspire others to persevere in keeping Sabbath too.

READ

(For context: Between the time of Moses until the end of the Israelites captivity, there were approximately seventy occasions in which the sabbatical year had been violated).

This is exactly the message of GOD that Jeremiah had preached: the desolate land put to an extended sabbath rest, a seventy-year Sabbath rest making up for all the unkept Sabbaths.
2 Chronicles 36: 21, MSG

MEDITATE

Take a few minutes to meditate on the words in the passage. Are there particular phrases or specific words standing out? Share what is being highlighted for you personally with your Circle. For further insight, ponder the questions and insert your perspective in the conversation.

Despite the commandment of the Sabbath, the Israelites continued to plough and sow in the seventh year. They refused to allow the land to rest so God would make it rest despite their disobedience. How is this Old Testament story relevant for us today?

What is God saying to us about the wilderness?

How might He be using a barren season for your good?

Name some people in your life or in the Bible who display grit.

How does their resolve inform your faith and choices?

What would it take for you to be a person characterized by grit when it comes to Sabbath?

PRAY

Spend a few minutes in silence and wait on the Lord.

CONTEMPLATE

Write down whatever comes to mind in the whitespace below. It can be a word, sentence, question, scripture verse, random thought, or image. Nothing is insignificant and everything is useful for capturing God's still small voice. When appropriate, share what comes from that time in your Circle. Perhaps what is discerned through listening prayer will be a gift for someone in the room.

CLOSING PRAYER

Dear Lord, forgive us when we have overlooked the Sabbath and continued to make time about productivity rather than holy rest. May our rest honor you. Give each of us an extra portion of grit to persevere in rest despite interruptions and temptations. Remind us that accomplishment is not a measurement of worth, but evidence of your faithfulness and love that trumps everything in this world. Amen!

RESPONSES FROM THE SABBATH SOCIETY

Your reflection today was particularly meaningful for me. For months, my husband has been very ill. It was the darkest time we've ever experienced. It wasn't anything life threatening, he just took a very long time to heal. Last Sunday he finally turned the corner and is on his way back to health. Many times, I felt as though I was wandering in the desert. Every morning I would pray and do my best to be grateful for the many good things that were happening, but sometimes I felt worn out with worry and prayers sounded hollow. It was during this time that I discovered the Sabbath Society and I read some of the books you recommended. That, along with the other components of my spiritual life, sustained me. I have lived long enough to know that it is in the darkest times when our faith is strengthened. It can't be any other way. We can't avoid suffering, but we can use it for good. Thank you for the reminder.

I have to admit, I don´t know that I ever read 2 Chronicles that deliberately before. I got out my study Bible and cross referenced. It went to Leviticus 26:40-45, where God remembered his covenant and restored his people despite their sin. He allowed time for the land to catch up with the people, even though it looked completely different. And doesn´t he still do that now? It´s been good to meditate on that this week.

I've been in a desolate place health-wise for over 22 years, but three years ago, He began to show me how I needed to completely surrender to His will. Rhythms of Rest came at exactly the right time - God's time! My symptoms matter not! Yes, I am dependent on low level heat on my back, and I need 8-10 hours sleep every night. There are other requirements for me to feel somewhat comfortable and to sleep well. Allowing my life to lay fallow while He joined me in my wilderness has taught me to listen to Him. Of course, I'm still learning. It's a life-long process. By resting in the best way for me, that's where I truly meet God!

Suddenly, I find my Sabbath-fueled weekends and quiet spaces through the week filled with "what now, Lord? I sense the story is changing." And so, more than ever, I need to keep practicing rest and the principles of Sabbath. I am experiencing a new kind of waiting, a new kind of testing, while He reveals what to do with all of this, and while I discover how this new found perspective from Him can be used to serve others.

Your words could not have come at a better time. I have had a challenging few days and was wondering how Sabbath was going to happen this week, so I asked God to help me see with my heart rather than my 'to do' list. I see now I need grit to persevere with Sabbath – I need it even more after this week! My soul and body need a reprieve.

He is Risen. And that's
why we can declare,
"Life is good."

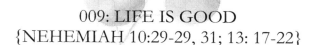

009: LIFE IS GOOD
{NEHEMIAH 10:29-29, 31; 13: 17-22}

While in Ohio for a writer's retreat, imagine my surprise when I discovered that many of the participants were also members of the Sabbath Society. One-by-one, people introduced themselves, telling personal stories about how the weekly Sabbath letters of encouragement make a difference in their world. We formed ourselves into a group after dinner one evening and captured the memory on film; Sabbath-keepers on retreat seemed appropriate somehow.

While my letters normally slip into inboxes all over the world every Friday, there is one Friday in the year that is different. On the liturgical calendar, Good Friday means more to us than an end of the week celebration and preparation for Sabbath. We cross over from 'good' as a casual, familiar response to the sobering reality of our sinfulness. And not one of us likes to be reminded of where we have fallen short.

But on Good Friday we need to remember that Jesus bore the weight of our sin nailed to a cross. As the world remembers Jesus' sacrifice on the same day every year, the fourth commandment asks us to remember His faithfulness through rest one day a week. Remember the Sabbath day, to keep it holy (Exodus 20:8).

I believe the fourth commandment begins with remember because we are prone to forget that rest isn't a prize for the result of good work, but a gift from God's generous, good, and loving heart. Remembering shifts our tendency toward self-reliance to putting things back to a reliance on God again.

"Well done, good and faithful servant. You have been faithful over a little; I will set you over much. Enter into the joy of your master." (Matthew 23:25) I would love to hear Jesus utter those words while looking at me, wouldn't you?!

Maybe you have started practicing Sabbath only to have compromise creep into your rhythm and desecrate your good intentions. You are resting half-heartedly, waiting to insert yourself back into the action at any minute. Your heart isn't really into complete rest. I understand.

On the first morning back home in London, after a long day of travel, I walked into the kitchen and was greeted with rice sticking to the bottom of slippers, crumbs decorating the counter tops. A list of forgotten grocery items was steeping in my head in tandem with the tea bag in my cup. First thoughts were of all the ways I've fallen short and all the things I've left undone. Sitting down with a warm cup in hand, I watch birds flit from branch to branch, and suddenly, remember why I am here. I whisper, "Thank you for breath and my daily bread."

He is Risen. And that's why we can declare, "Life is good."

READ

The rest of the people, the priests, the Levites, the gatekeepers, the singers, the temple servants, and all who have separated themselves from the peoples of the lands to the Law of God, their wives, their sons, their daughters, all who have knowledge and understanding, join with their brothers, their nobles, and enter into a curse and an oath to walk in God's Law that was given by Moses the servant of God, and to observe and do all the commandments of the Lord our Lord and his rules and his statutes. We will not give our daughters to the peoples of the land or take their daughters for our sons. And if the peoples of the land bring in goods or any grain on the Sabbath day to sell, we will not buy from them on the Sabbath or on a holy day. And we will forego the crops of the seventh year and the exaction of every debt.
Nehemiah 10:28-31

Then I confronted the nobles of Judah and said to them, "What is this evil thing that you are doing, profaning the Sabbath day? Did not your fathers act in this way, and did not our God bring all this disaster on us and on this city? Now you are bringing more wrath on Israel by profaning the Sabbath." As soon as it began to grow dark at the gates of Jerusalem before the Sabbath, I commanded that the doors should be shut and gave orders that they should not be opened until after the Sabbath. And I stationed some of my servants at the gates, that no load might be brought in on the Sabbath day. Then the merchants and sellers of all kinds of wares lodged outside Jerusalem once or twice. But I warned them and said to them, "Why do you lodge outside the wall? If you do so again, I will lay hands on you." From that time on they did not come on the Sabbath. Then I commanded the Levites that they should purify themselves and come and guard the gates, to keep the Sabbath day holy. Remember this also in my favor, O my God, and spare me according to the greatness of your steadfast love.
Nehemiah 13:17-22

MEDITATE

Take a few minutes to meditate on the words in the passage. Are there particular phrases or specific words standing out? Share what is being highlighted for you personally with your Circle. For further insight, ponder the questions and insert your perspective in the conversation.

Let's remember why God made the Sabbath a commandment and not a suggestion. What does it tell you about rest, that God commanded it? Do you translate rest as optional? What else did he command, and what does it tell you about the importance of Sabbath?

What desecrates Sabbath for you?

How does choosing Sabbath set you apart from the world?

What activity purifies your heart from stress?

How can you make time extraordinary on Sabbath this week?

PRAY

Spend a few minutes in silence and wait on the Lord.

CONTEMPLATE

Write down whatever comes to mind in the whitespace below. It can be a word, sentence, question, scripture verse, random thought, or image. Nothing is insignificant and everything is useful for capturing God's still small voice. When appropriate, share what comes from that time in your Circle. Perhaps what is discerned through listening prayer will be a gift for someone in the room.

CLOSING PRAYER

Lord, forgive me when I profane the time I choose for rest by making time ordinary. Help me to stay steadfast in my resolve to rest when I am prone to slip back into producing. Let me remember that what I lack in the moment is yours to fill with your goodness. The most important aspect of rest is intimacy with you. May the outcome of what I produce on Sabbath be deeper trust and confident love in our relationship. Amen!

Responses from the Sabbath Society

Finally, I am writing to you after joining the Sabbath Society last year and reading your book with the on-line book club. Sabbath became exciting after a lifetime of thinking it was otherwise. Thanks for opening my eyes to another of Gods great gifts to us. My Sabbaths have improved. Now I look forward to a quieter, simpler day, doing fun things, worshipping at church, and just enjoying the place where God has put me and the people he has given me. The dishwasher gets put to good use, the washing machine has a holiday, and meals are easy and hassle free.

On Sunday afternoons I've been reading Rhythms of Rest. *I began implementing small changes several weeks ago now. This Sunday caught me by surprise, but not because I wasn't ready. For the first time that I can remember, Resurrection Sunday was a day of pure celebration, not stressfully running from one thing to another. When I sat in my seat, I habitually went through my mental check list to be sure I hadn't forgotten anything. There wasn't a thing! I couldn't believe it -- it felt too good to be true. Surely there was something. Nope. I had kept things so simple, that I could rest in my sweet Savior and worship Him freely without being distracted by something I'd forgotten. It was a wonderful gift!*

Reading your message today was a sober reminder that in the last couple of 'extra busy' weeks, I have not made space to receive God's gift of rest as I should. This has landed me with the flu, and I am absolutely resting now!

Most of us have everything we need at our finger tips. So why do we struggle with rest?

010: WHAT DO YOU WANT?
{PSALM 23}

On Thursday evenings during the cold winter months, I stuff an apron into my coat pocket and walk to St. Barnabas Church in the dark. Once there, I tie the apron around my waist and insert myself among familiar faces standing around a large metal table of cutting boards, peelers, knives, vegetables and fresh herbs. Some are folding napkins, buttering slices of bread, and filling empty water pitchers with an orange flavored drink, transforming the renovated crypt into a dining room for homeless guests. Among the forty homeless guests that eat dinner with us regularly, we have become known for the most delicious meals in the circuit. They tell us this repeatedly while extending empty plates, asking for seconds and thirds.

After the chopping is finished, meals are served on plates, dessert is savored and dishes are mostly washed, I trade the apron for my wool coat and scarf in preparation for making the blustery trip back home. As I zig zag through the dining room to avoid people stacking chairs and folding tables, I wave goodbye to guests spending the night. Many have stretched out in a corner or next to a wall, eyes closed and drifting off to sleep.

Bright lights blaze and people chat in circles. A vacuum is pushed over a crumby floor, around many already cocooned in sleeping bags. Our homeless guests are weary and from necessity, they have learned how to rest anywhere, and at any time. No black out curtains or white noise needed.

As I return home, warmth greets me. I slip out of boots and into slippers and massage soap into hands under a hot tap. I spread out underneath a warm blanket in front of the television and think about what I will cook tomorrow for dinner from the plethora of choices stored in the refrigerator.

Most of us have everything we need at our finger tips. So why do we struggle with rest?

READ

The Lord is my shepherd; I shall not want. He makes me lie down in green pastures. He leads me beside still waters. He restores my soul. He leads me in paths of righteousness for his name's sake. Even though I walk through the valley of the shadow of death, I will fear no evil, for you are with me; your rod and your staff, they comfort me. You prepare a table before me in the presence of my enemies; you anoint my head with oil; my cup overflows. Surely goodness and mercy shall follow me all the days of my life, and I shall dwell in the house of the Lord forever.
Psalm 23

MEDITATE

Take a few minutes to meditate on the words in the following passage. Are there particular phrases or specific words standing out? Share what is being highlighted for you personally with your circle. For further insight, ponder the questions and insert your perspective in the conversation.

As you ponder each line in Psalm 23, read it in the context of someone in need, and then read it again for yourself.
What is a shepherd?

David writes, "The Lord my shepherd?" How does that personal intimacy inform your relationship with Jesus?

How does having a shepherd in charge of your life change your perspective on the unmet needs of your life?

Is it wrong to want? Explain your answer.

What does David mean when he says, I shall not want?

PRAY

Spend a few minutes in silence and wait on the Lord.

CONTEMPLATE

Write down whatever comes to mind in the whitespace below. It can be a word, sentence, question, scripture verse, random thought, or image. Nothing is insignificant and everything is useful for capturing God's still small voice. When appropriate, share what comes from that time in your Circle. Perhaps what is discerned through listening prayer will be a gift for someone in the room.

CLOSING PRAYER

Use the following lyrics of *I Shall Not Want* by Audrey Assad[4] as a closing prayer.

From the love of my own comfort
From the fear of having nothing
From a life of worldly passions
Deliver me O God

From the need to be understood
And from a need to be accepted
From the fear of being lonely
Deliver me O God
Deliver me O God

And I shall not want, no, I shall not want
When I taste Your goodness, I shall not want
When I taste Your goodness, I shall not want

From the fear of serving others
Oh, and from the fear of death or trial
And from the fear of humility
Deliver me O God
Yes, deliver me O God

And I shall not want, no, I shall not want
When I taste Your goodness, I shall not want

Responses from the Sabbath Society

Recently, I was thinking about how I slept and woke up when I was a child in my mother and father's home--with no concerns except for the present day. That changed as I grew older, more responsible, became the mother... But I am a child of God, and I can rest in him!

Tomorrow marks the end of an annual intense season for me, the season of directing students in a play. I was realizing how key that choice to slip into rest has been for my sanctity, my spiritual health, and my family life. Until your encouragement to rest became a part of my life, I was bringing a whole lot more stress into the situation. God is, indeed, good.

This week I contacted 23 acquaintances whom I know have wayward children. We have decided to share a verse of Scripture once a month and pray for each other's children. When it comes to the salvation of your children, there can be so much striving going on. But we know that it is not up to us but up to Him, who is able and full of mercy. I pray that in the midst of these prayers God will give us rest, rest in Him. And (listening to the Audrey Assad song 'I shall not want') I pray that He will deliver our children and us too.

I felt so touched by this week's newsletter. It bought tears to my eyes to remember that compared to a homeless person I have plenty materially even if there have been challenges. Yet, it seems to me, a homeless person may be richer in some ways than I am as they trust wholeheartedly to be fed, have a place to sleep and stay warm one day at a time. It's a reminder that the Lord is indeed our Shepherd and I shall not be in want no matter what each day brings, He is enough.

We can only trust God with our time to the degree we trust ourselves as stewards with the time he gives. God is good, even when life disappoints you.

011: GRIEVING A DIFFERENT ENDING
{PSALM 90}

For months, I've been sitting with the story of the Exodus in the Old Testament. There is so much to learn from the life of Moses and the story of the Israelites wandering through the desert. And clarity cannot be rushed. What God wants to teach you cannot be hurried into paragraphs or read like a check list. Savoring words moves one from an acquaintance of God to deep friendship. And like Moses, I want to be called a friend of God, don't you?

As I read Numbers 20, the story of Moses' siblings, Miriam and Aaron, I wept over their passing. All that time travelling as a family, experiencing God's miracles, leading, loving, and influencing people together, and none of them would enter the Promised Land. I knew the familiar story, but meditating on the words and their meaning, information in my head morphed into truth penetrating the heart. Sometimes we must grieve a different ending. But a different ending doesn't mean God has changed his mind about you. God is sovereign, even in our disappointment.

Life doesn't always pan out the way we hope or envision and grief is natural in the wake of disappointment. An immediate response to unexpected endings begins as shock, often followed with the familiar question, Why would God allow that to happen? For me, the answer comes by way of Psalm 90, the only psalm scholars attribute to Moses.

It is a psalm dealing with the darker side of life; the pain of living in holy anticipation only to be disappointed by outcomes. The first ten verses communicate the plight of man: the things we are remiss to acknowledge about the realities of life. And the remaining verses encapsulate Moses' petition – teach us, come back to us, show us your glory, make what we do successful. There are lots of exclamation points in those verses that translate as pleading. So, teach us to number our days that we may get a heart of wisdom (verse 12). This is the very reason why we practice a rhythm of rest each week.

Like Moses, we need to see life as it is and ourselves as God sees us. We must acknowledge that God is eternal and man is mortal; God is righteous and man is sinful. To deny the dark side of life is to diminish the power of the Light to save us. We need God more than He needs us. We can only see ourselves as we really are when we come to see God as He really is. We can only trust God with our time to the degree we trust ourselves as stewards with the time he gives. God is good, even when life disappoints you.

God insists over and over again that we move our eyes upward; from the small things that keep us stuck to the big, sweeping stories he is writing for us. As we rest, abide, listen, move out, and look up, we are surprised by the beauty that is cultivated, like stumbling onto a burning bush while wandering in the grocery store. Even in our disappointment we can still exclaim, "Glory!"

READ

Lord, you have been our dwelling place in all generations. Before the mountains were brought forth, or ever you had formed the earth and the world, from everlasting to everlasting you are God. You return man to dust and say, "Return, O children of man!" For a thousand years in your sight are but as yesterday when it is past, or as a watch in the night. You sweep them away as with a flood; they are like a dream, like grass that is renewed in the morning: in the morning it flourishes and is renewed; in the evening it fades and withers. For we are brought to an end by your anger; by your wrath we are dismayed. You have set our iniquities before you, our secret sins in the light of your presence. For all our days pass away under your wrath; we bring our years to an end like a sigh. The years of our life are seventy, or even by reason of strength eighty; yet their span is but toil and trouble; they are soon gone, and we fly away. Who considers the power of your anger, and your wrath according to the fear of you? So teach us to number our days that we may get a heart of wisdom. Return, O Lord! How long? Have pity on your servants! Satisfy us in the morning with your steadfast love, that we may rejoice and be glad all our days. Make us glad for as many days as you have afflicted us, and for as many years as we have seen evil. Let your work be shown to your servants, and your glorious power to their children. Let the favor of the Lord our God be upon us, and establish the work of our hands upon us; yes, establish the work of our hands!
Psalm 90

MEDITATE

Take a few minutes to meditate on the words in the passage. Are there particular phrases or specific words standing out? Share what is being highlighted for you personally with your Circle. For further insight, ponder the questions and insert your perspective in the conversation.

What preferred ending are you holding onto that you need to release into God's care?

What projected ending are you grieving that hasn't happened yet?

What disappointment do you need to resolve as closure in order to move forward into what God has for you?

Write verses of petition as an offering of surrender. How does that exercise change your perspective?

PRAY

Spend a few minutes in silence and wait on the Lord.

CONTEMPLATE

Write down whatever comes to mind in the whitespace below. It can be a word, sentence, question, scripture verse, random thought, or image. Nothing is insignificant and everything is useful for capturing God's still small voice. When appropriate, share what comes from that time in your Circle. Perhaps what is discerned through listening prayer will be a gift for someone in the room.

CLOSING PRAYER

Lord, I am prone to define dark periods as a lack of your favor or a result of my failure. Lead me to the truth. I want to follow your presence. Help me to see where your Light shines amidst the darkness. Guide my thoughts when I am blinded by self-reliance. Though I suffer with disappointments, your hope does not disappoint. Like Moses, may I fulfill your purposes and bring you glory through perseverance, even when inner rest feels elusive. Amen!

RESPONSES FROM THE SABBATH SOCIETY

Your words resonate a lot today! I too was grieved for Moses as he came to the end of his earthly journey. Shortly after I met you in London, I had an early miscarriage - so early that I hadn't taken a test although I knew I would do so soon. I have a whole barrage of thoughts and feelings about the life that was so briefly inside me and has been safely delivered to heaven, but I am still wrestling through and processing a lot of them. It hasn't made me doubt him at all, I know that all the trials we go through are a beautiful opportunity to rest in him more closely. But the sadness comes in waves every so often and I wonder at the purpose.

Retiring at the beginning of the year, not quite knowing what to do with myself; a month of sickness; and now we have just returned from seeing our new grandbaby who is very far away (and I most certainly wish we were closer). I am a little at 'a loose end'. Your words were a great reminder that God is still in control and that as I rest in Him, I will find my answers and comfort there.

Your paragraph about denying the dark side of life is to diminish the power of the Light to save us, and about being good stewards of what He provides as timing... this all reminds me of what my pastor calls "holy tension". It's the darkness emphasizing Light's purpose. It's the give and take of our walk in Him. Spiritual balance takes this blend of waiting in Him and then pushing ahead when He gives the signal, no matter what else crops up in life. And when it gets too dark, we call on Him to shine bright, to light the path or the circumstance, or the questions. Lost in the desert and yet, Promise Land-bound all at once... a holy tension.

I just received news today that an offer we had put on a house was refused. I know that in the great scheme of things this does not feel like a big deal, but for us, right now, it does. My husband went through a six-month process of applying to different job openings in order to move to a warmer place, partly to help his depression. Although many of those options looked very promising, nothing came of them. One by one the doors closed. I was hoping that the acceptance of this house offer would confirm to him that we were meant to stay here, but now that is not happening. I guess I just don't have to feel responsible for him. He needs to walk through his own process of disappointment and come to terms with what the Lord is allowing in our lives.

Live as though you are loved, and God's abundance is the language you discern from the cacophony.

012: DELIGHT IN DETOURS
{ISAIAH 56:1-8 + 58:13}

On Saturday, I awakened with a bout of sneezing and wiping watery eyes, using boxes of Kleenex strategically located on every floor of the house. I hoped the onslaught of a runny nose was more about springtime pollen than catching the cold my son was nursing the week before. Weekend plans include miles of walking to and from a favorite farmers market in Notting Hill. Not only was I dreaming of the decadent fresh produce transported into the city by country farmers, I was also anticipating the inspiration of beauty while walking past rows of white terrace houses and floral gardens. A favorite path to meander with a camera hanging off my shoulder, the walk has become an anticipated activity as spring sunshine and warmth awakens a sullen winter landscape. But my body is issuing a warning about those pre-made plans in preparation for Sabbath.

As I paused to survey my walled garden from the window, I offer a simple prayer. *Lord, what I should do?* And clarity comes quickly. *Though you can walk those miles and enjoy the market, it will drain you for doing anything else the rest of the day. Is it worth it?*

I don't know about you, but the longer I sit with God, the more I've come to learn that he responds, not with clear concrete answers, but with more questions that allow me to choose. The longer I sit still and listen rather than plan and produce, the truth begins sounding a lot like wisdom. *You already have a nearly full refrigerator, you don't really need more of anything. Your phone is full of photos captured that you've yet to fully look at and edit.*

A pause before moving into action cleared a pathway for desire to bubble up to the surface. And desire translated differently than what I was originally cooking up. Sometimes we need to simmer in thought before truth can be digested and life fully savored. *What you are hungry for is light and warmth, feeling the wind on your skin and the sun on your legs, being inserted into the outer world after being alone and inside with your work all week. There are other ways of experiencing that that won't exhaust you.*

Alternatively, H and I walk a few steps from our front door to the neighborhood market. We carry home a tub of herbed olives, stuffed grape leaves, and loaf of crusty seeded bread and spread out the agrarian treasures on the table in the garden. As we pop olives into our mouths like candy, birds sing from the treetops swaying in a breeze above us, children's voices speaking French bounce off the stone walls, and a rhythmic thump, thump, thump from a basketball gives hints of a community gathering. A bumble bee buzzes like a mini-helicopter in a holding pattern above the crown of my head. Savoring each bite, the flavors and sounds satiate my hunger for a fresh and inspiring experience.

For thus says the Lord: "To the eunuchs who keep my Sabbaths, who choose the things that please me and hold fast my covenant, I will give in my house and within my walls a monument and a name better than sons and daughters; I will give them an everlasting name that shall not be cut off. (Isaiah 56: 4-5)." Eunuchs were considered outcasts, unable to fully participate in temple rituals. But God is letting even the eunuchs know that He has a name and a place for them in his house.

Feeling like a foreigner to God's voice can become a self-fulfilling prophecy. But live as though you are loved, and God's abundance is the language you discern from the cacophony. Soon, you speak it with fluency to those around you. You might feel like you are an outsider to God's promises; an outcast to the abundant life you witness in others. But God says you belong, so you must trust Him. You can rest because you are deeply loved and fully known.

In this world fraught with uncertainty, hear hope echoing off the stone walls of your complicated circumstances. Your only certainty is God's presence with you working all things together for your good, even when you can't hear or see the evidence. Sabbath is an awakening of the soul to spiritual springtime.

READ

Thus says the Lord: "Keep justice, and do righteousness, for soon my salvation will come, and my righteousness be revealed. Blessed is the man who does this, and the son of man who holds it fast, who keeps the Sabbath, not profaning it, and keeps his hand from doing any evil." Let not the foreigner who has joined himself to the Lord say, "The Lord will surely separate me from his people"; and let not the eunuch say, "Behold, I am a dry tree." For thus says the Lord: "To the eunuchs who keep my Sabbaths, who choose the things that please me and hold fast my covenant, I will give in my house and within my walls a monument and a name better than sons and daughters; I will give them an everlasting name that shall not be cut off. "And the foreigners who join themselves to the Lord, to minister to him, to love the name of the Lord, and to be his servants, everyone who keeps the Sabbath and does not profane it, and holds fast my covenant— these I will bring to my holy mountain, and make them joyful in my house of prayer; their burnt offerings and their sacrifices will be accepted on my altar; for my house shall be called a house of prayer for all peoples." The Lord God, who gathers the outcasts of Israel, declares, "I will gather yet others to him besides those already gathered."
Isaiah 56:1-8

"If you turn back your foot from the Sabbath, from doing your pleasure on my holy day, and call the Sabbath a delight and the holy day of the Lord honorable; if you honor it, not going your own ways, or seeking your own pleasure, or talking idly; then you shall take delight in the Lord."
Isaiah 58: 13-14 (I suggest reading this one in the Message!)

MEDITATE

Take a few minutes to meditate on the words in the passage. Are there particular phrases or specific words standing out? Share what is being highlighted for you personally with your Circle. For further insight, ponder the questions and insert your perspective in the conversation.

If you were to pause and listen to your life for a few moments, what would you hear?

What are you holding onto that might allow you to rest if you were to let go and let God lead you?

How might an unexpected detour be God's opportunity to re-route you toward providence?

This week, take five minutes and sit somewhere alone with a notebook and pen. Write down all the things you hear. And then ask God to reveal what you've been missing.

PRAY

Spend a few minutes in silence and wait on the Lord.

CONTEMPLATE

Write down whatever comes to mind in the whitespace below. It can be a word, sentence, question, scripture verse, random thought, or image. Nothing is insignificant and everything is useful for capturing God's still small voice. When appropriate, share what comes from that time in your Circle. Perhaps what is discerned through listening prayer will be a gift for someone in the room.

CLOSING PRAYER

Lord, when I am bent on a plan, help me to live open-handed. Help me to think of detours as your best, rather than a busted day. Reveal to us this week where we've made wrong assumptions about how life should look. Help us to listen to our lives before rushing into assumptions. Give us big, bold perspective that allows us to rest fully in the fullness of a full and vibrant life. Amen!

RESPONSES FROM THE SABBATH SOCIETY

For weeks, I have been in a place of waking up in the morning and just spending time listening to what God's saying and writing in my journal. He said to me about two and a half months ago that I need to come into his presence, speak less and listen more. It's the reason why he's given us two ears and one mouth! Out of these precious times have come clarity, direction and of course, always, the outpouring of his love.

Sabbath is really a kindness to us, isn't it? Oh, how often I treat myself harshly when God's intentions & messages are light & grace-giving!

I have been a Christian for many years, and grew up in a Christian home. But Sabbath has never really been on my mind until now. I am amazed by all the passages that there are in the Bible about Sabbath. I admit, before I started thinking more about it, I never realized what God really says about it. I knew Sabbath was important, but just kind of brushed it off, I guess.

The passage for this week really spoke to me. Sabbath is about finding joy in the Lord. He has everything that we need and he wants to give it to us. How often I forget that! And there is a reason why he gives us the Sabbath, because he knows we need it. We can't do it in our own strength. And that, I realize, is often what I have been trying to do. Also, it's about pausing and really listening for what God is saying to me in the moments of my day. Taking the time to "simmer in thought", as you put it, so that truth can come. Still trying to figure out how to do that more.

Sabbath is like being kissed with a promise, loved without striving, accepted for just being you.

013: SABBATH AS A SIGN
{EZEKIEL 20:12-13}

On Saturday, I awakened to H holding a tray decorated with an egg and toast breakfast, making eye contact with a serious request. *Do not do anything but get ready for the day ahead.* We had plans for dinner at our favorite Italian restaurant in celebration of our 28th wedding anniversary, but I had no idea what else he was up to. But because of his track record, I knew whatever he was planning would be thoughtful, generous, and kind. Especially when he casually remarked, *You might want to bring your camera with you.*

In the early years of our union, his secret plans scared me. I know that may sound crazy, but an insecure childhood made me wary of surprises and risk averse. Uncertainty created a vacuum of trust and shamed me into thinking I'm not enough. But over the years, H has rescued me from fear by proving himself trustworthy. Belonging often comes before we believe.

Like the wedding ring I wear on my finger as a symbol of commitment to H, Sabbath is a sign between us and God of covenant relationship--holy, set apart, and different. As I meditate on the scripture passage in Ezekiel, I think of God's unrequited love for the Israelites, and their ungrateful attitude to his generous gift of Sabbath. As if I responded to H's thoughtfulness with, "Oh no! I'm not having it. I had things planned today, lists to check off and people to see. I don't have time to wander around London with you."

In the very wilderness where God performed countless miracles in response to the whining of Israelites, they still doubted his goodness and faithfulness. They refused to believe what he was saying was trustworthy, even though God had proven himself over and over again. As I take a personal inventory, I see that I am not as open and trusting as I would like to think I am. You?

How many times have you been told by someone that you are beautiful but didn't believe it?

How many times have you known you needed to stop and rest but didn't believe you could do it?

How many times have you read an email from me and chose to believe Sabbath is for all those other people and not you?

I admit, when H tells me I'm beautiful, I'm prone to point out that little jiggle in my thighs instead of saying, "Thank you." I declare a litany of things left undone instead of focusing on the mountain of good things accomplished. I witness the productivity and prosperity of others only to create a list of the things I lack and the ways I fall short.

If we only measure the value of time by what we lack, then we miss the abundance of God's goodness staring us in the face. Seeing the shadows without capturing the light does some damage to hope within us. If Sabbath is a means of becoming holy then it is in rest, not our productivity, that we find true happiness, today and eternally. In *Rhythms of the Inner Life*, Howard Macy was on to something when he wrote, "I don't know anyone who is terminally grumpy and is also genuinely happy."[5]

As I stood on the platform next to H, waiting for a train to arrive with camera hanging over my shoulder and sunglasses on my face, a hint to where we were going appeared on the map. "Are we going to Kew Gardens?" I exclaimed.

A smile on his face was my answer. H doesn't find deep fulfillment in walking through parks and looking at flowers. He isn't inspired in the same way I am to take a million pictures. He is fulfilled in being present and enjoying the experience of witnessing my happiness. And isn't that the same posture Jesus carries with each of us? There are no caveats, hoops to jump through, addendums to how love is supposed to look, or preambles for acceptance.

Sabbath is like being kissed with a promise, loved without striving, accepted for just being you. Celebrate your relationship with Jesus and believe that you are loved for who you are and not what you do.

READ

And I gave them my Sabbath days of rest as a sign between them and me. It was to remind them that I am the Lord, who had set them apart to be holy. But the people of Israel rebelled against me, and they refused to obey my decrees there in the wilderness. They wouldn't obey my regulations even though obedience would have given them life. They also violated my Sabbath days. So I threatened to pour out my fury on them, and I made plans to utterly consume them in the wilderness. Ezekiel 20:12-13

MEDITATE

Take a few minutes to meditate on the words in the following passage. Are there particular phrases or specific words standing out? Share what is being highlighted for you personally with your Circle. For further insight, ponder the questions and insert your perspective in the conversation.

How does seeing Sabbath as a sign of God's commitment to you change your perspective about rest?

How does time without productivity translate for you?

In what areas are you lacking trust that Sabbath is God's gift to you?

What makes you worthy of rest? And worthy of love?

Make a list of what you have as an answer for what you lack and surrender it as a love letter to Jesus.

Pray

Spend a few minutes in silence and wait on the Lord.

Contemplate

Write down whatever comes to mind in the whitespace below. It can be a word, sentence, question, scripture verse, random thought, or image. Nothing is insignificant and everything is useful for capturing God's still small voice. When appropriate, share what comes from that time in your Circle. Perhaps what is discerned through listening prayer will be a gift for someone in the room.

CLOSING PRAYER

Lord, forgive me for the ways I assign value to myself outside of our relationship. Give me the courage to accept myself as lovable and desirable regardless of what I produce. I relinquish the need to prove myself as a sign of worthiness. Forgive me. Thank you for the sign of your faithful love and presence through the gift of Sabbath. May my heart, mind, and soul rest in the truth of your purity and goodness. Amen!

RESPONSES FROM THE SABBATH SOCIETY

Gah! Once again so, so good. I was sitting here, reeling from some disappointing news, but then I was reminded how Jesus is trustworthy and so are His ways, even if it looks different than I thought.

"Uncertainty created a vacuum of trust and shamed me into thinking I'm not enough." That really helped me recognize an issue, something I'm hesitant to release to God. I had an unstable childhood and I hate surprises. I hadn't considered that connection or how my dislike of surprises is a way I have placed walls around myself. As I read Rhythms of Rest last summer I was convicted of how certainty is an idol in my life and God has been quietly moving in my life helping me see more ways in which this idol has entangled itself in so much of me... and here is another way I hadn't seen yet. In a little 'promise notebook' I write for myself I've put your quote, "Trust that God's plans for you are good" and let Him surprise me. It is a scary word for me, but important in realizing how fully I am accepted by Him and how to live in the freedom of His joy and rest.

Thanks for your honest transparency. I'd never before thought about the insecurities I harbored all of my adolescent and young adult years might make me averse to surprises! Something new to ponder. But mostly it was revealing to me that in this season of busy Sundays-- when I generally take my Sabbath rest--I had only been sneaking in little bits and pieces. Until this week. I had one day when the only things on my schedule were a haircut (personal pampering) and lunch with a friend. As I jotted down the events of the day, I realized that I had treated the day like a Sabbath--not squeezing in extra errands or making a to do list. It feels like I am understanding the importance of Sabbath without being tied to it.

I felt like I was right there with you as you described your day with H. I, too, have been rescued by love through my husband and I often feel the very real and palpable love of Jesus through his gentleness with me. The concept of Sabbath as a gift from someone who is utterly in love with you is like looking at it through the slightly altered view of a beautiful kaleidoscope. There are so many facets to the idea of Sabbath - so much more than just a set of rules. It's like a cool glass of water in the shade of a summer day.

Sabbath isn't miraculous, it's a miracle of God's great love revealed in you.

014: BREAKING SCHEMAS
{EZEKIEL 20:20}

At the time of writing this, Londoners are twenty-four hours away from witnessing the big royal wedding between Prince Harry and Meghan Markle. It's all terribly exciting and hopeful. While headlines communicate uncertainties around the world, the union between a prince and an American actress give hope that our schemas for life can be beautifully broken. They give the world hope that impossible dreams are possible and happy endings aren't just for fairy tales.

As we end this Old Testament series of Sabbath reflections, I thought it appropriate to share an inspiring letter received from a brand new Sabbath Society member that breaks many of the schemas we have about rest, especially for those in the season of raising little people when margin is slim.

A schema is a general conception for something that is common to all of us. For instance: If you practice Sabbath that means you can't do anything but nap or lay in a hammock all day. Jesus broke a common religious schema when he healed a shriveled hand on the Sabbath, a taboo for those of Pharisaical mindsets.

And for those of you who struggle with little margin for rest, this letter I'm sharing with you communicates proof that your hope about making rest a rhythm of life can be realized beyond wishful thinking. Sabbath isn't for all those other fortunate people, it is for you too!

I have so enjoyed my last 6 months in the Sabbath Society. A friend and fellow Sabbath-keeper is one of my nearest and dearest and she has quietly been loving and resting in Sabbath for the past five years. I've watched and nodded from the sidelines and thought, "How nice for her - perhaps when my children are older." And then last August my life felt heavy. Add the oppressive Phoenix heat, a remodel, two little girls four and under, and the sameness of summer routine together and it all took me to a depressed and dry spot. I was in the Word, continuing to attend church, plugging away at my life as a work-from-home mom... but I was dying on the inside and I couldn't explain why. I tried to explain it away with the season.

Bible studies started, fall speaking and teaching sessions picked up and yet I still couldn't shake the monotony. I felt it especially on the weekends. I would almost dread them. While they meant relief for my husband, it felt as though my work was never, ever done. I didn't get to rest. I would never get to rest. My life was aching for a new rhythm and a deep rest. Enter the picture in my mind of my friend's "Sabbath cart" with paper products (used for meals to avoid cleaning dirty dishes) thinking about her family enjoying their Sabbath pizza together. Perhaps there was something to it. We've talked about needing and wanting Sabbath but just couldn't practically figure it out.

And then I picked up your book and Mark Buchanan's Rest of God over Christmas break. I signed up for the Sabbath Society even before I practiced any of it. I'd switched off all social media at weekends during the fall - a welcome change and a good start. In car rides, I shared all I was learning with my husband. I listened to multiple podcast episodes on the topic of rest and Sabbath and came away with a new understanding.

1. Rest was not earned. It was a gift.

2. As your post from last week echoed— it's a symbol of my relationship with the Lord.

3. Practicing weekly Sabbath is not only an act of obedience and worship, but an act of release and dependence.

This past year has been so good for my soul. We kicked off the year wanting to discover how our weekends could shift – how the tone could change. I love where we've ended up. Release of social media. Pizza and movie picnics on Friday. Family activity Saturday morning and then an afternoon full of chores and Sabbath prep. Sunday: church - slow to leave! We used to rush to Costco. Now we linger. Home for outdoor lunch and the kids play in the water table while we read and dream. Rest time - the kids nap/rest while we read books and fall asleep on the couches. Then a trip to the library or park before a casual dinner. It is my most favorite day of the week. How fitting that the Lord starts our week with rest!

Maybe you don't have children to keep you from intentional rest, but you can relate to that "dying on the inside" feeling our friend writes about. You know you need to rest, but you can't figure out how to make rest a reality in your busy life. Can I encourage you to just begin? If you don't make changes, nothing changes in your life. This series is the beginning of the Sabbath-keeping journey for some of you and an encouragement to carry on for others. But taking the leap is where the magic happens and life begins to deepen with purpose and meaning. Sabbath isn't miraculous, it's a miracle of God's great love revealed in you.

READ

Keep my Sabbath days holy, for they are a sign to remind you that I am the Lord your God.
Ezekiel 20:20, NIV

MEDITATE

Take a few minutes to meditate on the words in the passage. Are there particular phrases or specific words standing out? Share what is being highlighted for you personally with your Circle. For further insight, ponder the questions and insert your perspective in the conversation.

How can you turn desire for rest into actionable Sabbath?

What is one small step you can you take that deepens your relationship with God through rest?

What are your Sabbath schemas—common conceptions mistakenly adopted—that need to be broken?

How have those misconceptions squelched creativity in rest?

Plan a conversation about Sabbath with the people who live under your roof. Share about how each of you enjoy rest. Create your individual rhythms of rest. Support each other in preparation.

PRAY

As you close this session on the Old Testament, spend a few minutes in silence and wait on the Lord. Allow the Holy Spirit to guide your thoughts toward the truth pondered in your Circle.

CONTEMPLATE

Write down whatever comes to mind in the whitespace below. It can be a previous reflection captured; a simple word, sentence, question, or scripture verse brought back to your attention. Nothing is insignificant and everything is useful for capturing God's still small voice. When appropriate, share what comes from that time in your Circle. Perhaps what is discerned through listening prayer will be a gift for someone in the room.

CLOSING PRAYER

Lord, take all we've learned in this Sabbath Society Circle and imprint the truth on our hearts. Help us to take away those things that are helpful in persevering in rest and remove those things that keep us stuck and tired. Thank you for the relationships that have grown here through the theme of rest. We pray that as we separate for a season, your words will come back to us when we need them. Keep our resolve. May we be a support to one another, a listening ear and an empathetic shoulder. Continue the good work you have done among us. Amen!

RESPONSES FROM THE SABBATH SOCIETY

We're a week from my daughter's graduation and less than a week from moving into our newly renovated house. The theme this month in my small group is "BE WHERE YOU ARE." I chose it months ago thinking I wanted to be intentional about being present during these last few weeks of high school for my daughter. I had no idea the utter chaos we'd be living in! But God is so good, isn't he? He knew I'd need that daily reminder 'to be' where I am — whether it's packing or taking pictures at prom, senior walk or painting doors. It's been a gift to be present — to give myself permission to be in one place at a time. It's a discipline I could never have practiced without understanding true rest — the call to sudden and complete stops, the necessity of doing less so I can be more.

DEFINING TERMS

Lectio Divina — Read, Meditate, Pray, Contemplate.

Read scripture (1Corinthians 2: 9-10), perhaps several times (Romans 10: 8-10) in an atmosphere of stillness (Psalm 46:10).

Meditate on the passage without jumping to conclusions, giving the Holy Spirit space for revealing truth. Rather than analysis and dissecting words, peace is the purpose (John 14:27).

Pray for illumination (Psalm 119:105).

Contemplate God's love through silent prayer (Romans 5:8).

Listening Prayer—Taking the posture of receptivity. Wait on the Lord (Psalm 27:14 and Jeremiah 42:7). Relax and practice attentive listening, moving the focus away from things left undone to the person of Jesus. Release cares and receive God's love. When listening prayer is practiced in community, discernment during times of silence can often be a source of ministry for others. The details of what you receive may be for you, and also for someone in your Circle.

LEADING A CIRCLE

Read *Rhythms of Rest: Finding the Spirit of Sabbath in a Busy World* by Shelly Miller.

Subscribe to the Sabbath Society weekly email at www.shellymillerwriter.com.

Join the Sabbath Society Leader's Circle on Facebook and engage regularly.

Attend three of four quarterly Zoom calls for in-real life connection and leadership training.

Practice an ongoing weekly (albeit imperfect) rhythm of Sabbath-keeping.

Desire greater intimacy with Jesus.

Receptiveness to listen—in prayer, conversation, and reading scripture.

Willingness to practice vulnerable hospitality in the spirit of ease and togetherness.

Openness to participate in friendship evangelism, discipleship, and mentoring.

How to Curate a Sabbath Society Circle in Your Spheres of Influence

A Sabbath Society Circle can be as small as three people or as large as twelve. A Circle can be formed at work in a break room over lunch, or with friends on a Saturday at the park. In the living room of a friend's home around coffee and snacks, or wine and canapes. Gather people around a conference room after hours, or around the table for a meal in your home.

Circles are created for gathering online Sabbath Society community members for the purpose of being present with kindreds. But invitation extended to neighbors, co-workers, and friends in your community are also encouraged and welcomed. Each group is designed to be autonomous and specific to the culture and atmosphere where you live. People everywhere share weariness as the outcome of busyness, and you are providing space to pause and exhale regularly.

The frequency of your gathering is at your discretion—weekly, bi-weekly, or monthly. In my experience, the more frequently you meet in the initial launch, the quicker friendships deepen and become vulnerable.

Ground rules should be re-stated to the group frequently—refer to what a Sabbath Society Circle is and is not.

NOTES

1   Shelly Miller, Rhythms of Rest: Finding the Spirit of Sabbath in a Busy World, Bloomington, Minnesota, Bethany House, 2016, p.99-100.

2   Ruth Haley Barton, Sacred Rhythms: Arranging Our Lives for Spiritual Transformation, Downers Grove, IL, InterVarsity Press, 2009, page 132.

3   Angela Duckworth, Grit: The Power of Passion and Perseverance, London, England, Vermilion, 2016, (Quote from Duckworth's TED Talk).

4   Audrey Assad, I Shall Not Want, Fortunate Fall, 2013

5   Howard R. Macy, Rhythms of the Inner Life: Yearning for Closeness with God, Newberg, Oregon, Red Nose Fun Publishing, 1988, 1992, 1999, 2012, Loc 1724, Kindle.

ACKNOWLEDGMENTS

This book wouldn't be possible without the online Sabbath Society community. Thank you for a wealth of rich responses to weekly letters since 2013. I'm grateful for your support, encouragement and perseverance that make rest realistic and restorative.

To Helen Cockram, a wonderful editor: For your ability to think like a reader; curiosity to ask questions like a student; experience to edit as a professional—I'm completely indebted. Thank you for the fine tuning that make words sing.

For H, who champions my writing ideas and projects even when it means more work added to his already full plate. I'm thankful for your technical prowess and big picture questions that save me from stopping before beginning.

Thanks to my talented children—Harrison who created the cover design and Murielle who designed the logo for Sabbath Society Circles. Giving your time and thoughtful attention to the visual pieces required in birthing a new ministry is a great gift I will always cherish.

ABOUT THE AUTHOR

Shelly Miller is a veteran ministry leader and sought-after mentor on Sabbath keeping. She leads the Sabbath Society, an online community of people who want to make rest a priority. As a personal development coach, Shelly has learned the importance of asking good questions that lead to discovery, clarity, and ultimately, life transformation. Her writing has been featured in multiple books and national publications. Described as a poet with an acute taste for authentic honesty, she is a storyteller who makes people think differently about life. An expat living in London, England, she and her husband, H, are the proud parents of two adult children, Murielle and Harrison.

Find more of Shelly's writing, join the Sabbath Society community, and learn about personal development coaching at ShellyMillerWriter.com; Instagram and Twitter: @shellymillerwriter; Facebook: Shelly Miller, Writer. #SabbathSociety and #RhythmsofRest in community. For an inside look into new projects and London life, join Shelly's Patreon community at www.patreon.com/ShellyMiller.

Foreword by **Mark Buchanan**, author of *The Rest of God*

RHYTHMS *of* REST

Finding the Spirit *of* Sabbath in a Busy World

SHELLY MILLER

Manufactured by Amazon.ca
Bolton, ON

10896575R00094